Look what you've done now, Moses

Fredrick and Patricia McKissack
Illustrated by Joe Boddy

THIS I LOVE TO READ BOOK . . .

- has been carefully written to be fun and interesting for the young reader.
- repeats words over and over again to help the child read easily and to build the child's vocabulary.
- uses the lyrical rhythm and simple style that appeals to children.
- is told in the easy vocabulary of the validated word lists for 'grades one, two, and three from the *Ginn Word Book for Teachers: A Basic Lexicon.*
- is written to a mid-second grade reading level on the Fry Readability Test.

To Kaye Guynn

Chariot Books is an imprint of David C. Cook Publishing Co.
David C. Cook Publishing Co., Elgin, Illinois 60120
David C. Cook Publishing Co., Weston, Ontario

LOOK WHAT YOU'VE DONE NOW, MOSES
© 1984 by Fredrick and Patricia McKissack
Cover and interior illustrations by Joe Boddy
Printed in the United States of America
89 88 87 86 85 84   5 4 3 2 1

Library of Congress Cataloging in Publication Data
McKissack, Pat, 1944—
    Look what you've done now, Moses.
    1. Moses (Biblical leader)—Juvenile literature.
2. Bible. O.T.—Biography—Juvenile literature.
[1. Moses (Biblical leader) 2. Bible stories—O.T.]
I. McKissack, Fredrick. II. Boddy, Joe, ill.
III. Title.
BS580.M6M34 1984   222'.10924 [B]   83-23983
ISBN 0-89191-812-4 (pbk.)
ISBN 0-89191-839-6 (hc.)

Contents

Baby in a
basket

Long ago,

and far away,

at a time

after the beginning

after Noah and the Flood,

after Abraham and Isaac,

after Jacob and Joseph,

the children of Israel were slaves

in Egypt.

But Pharaoh was afraid of them.

There were so many Hebrew slaves.

So many men and women.

So many boys and girls.

Pharaoh thought of a bad plan.
"Kill all the Hebrew baby boys,"
he ordered.

Amram (AM-ram) and Jochebed
(JOCK-uh-bed) were Hebrew slaves.
They had a baby boy.
They kept the baby in secret
for a while.
But Jochebed knew she couldn't
hide him much longer.

So night after night
Jochebed put together reeds.

She wove them

in and out, in and out,

around and around,

in and out, in and out,

around and around.

Her daughter Miriam watched.

"What will you put in your basket?"

she asked.

"You will see," answered Jochebed.

Then she put tar around the bottom.

"Now the basket will float,"

Miriam said.

"What will you put in the basket?"

"You will see," answered Jochebed.

The next morning Jochebed put her baby boy in the basket.

Splash!

She put the basket in the Nile River.

"What will happen to my baby
brother?" Miriam asked.

"God will take care of him,"
said Jochebed.

And he did.

Miriam waited and watched.

Pharaoh's daughter found the basket.

"Oh, a baby!" she said.

Pharaoh's daughter did not have
a baby of her own.

"I will keep the baby," she said.

"He will be my son.

I will name him MOSES,

because I took him out of the water."

10   (Exodus 1: 8—Exodus 2: 10)

Who me?

The baby Moses grew older.

The baby Moses became a little boy.

The baby Moses grew to be a big boy.

The baby Moses grew to be

a young man.

One day Moses saw an Egyptian
beating a Hebrew slave.
The Egyptian was going to kill
the Hebrew.
Moses looked to the left.
Moses looked to the right.
He thought no one was looking.
He thought no one would tell.
He killed the Egyptian
to save the slave.
But someone did see Moses.
And someone even told Pharaoh.
Pharaoh was angry.
Moses had to run far, far away.

He ran to the land of Midian.

Finally he sat down by a well.

The seven daughters of Jethro came
to the well.

They had come to water their sheep.

But some shepherds stopped them.

"Step away," they said.

"We will water our sheep first."

Moses stood up.

"But the women were here first,"
Moses said.

"So what!" answered the shepherds.

Wham! Zap! Bam!

Moses beat the shepherds, and they ran away.

Moses stayed in Midian for 40 years.
He married Zipporah, one of Jethro's
7 daughters.
Moses was happy being a shepherd.
But God had other work for him.

One day Moses was watching
his sheep.
Crackle! Crackle! Crackle!
A bush near him was on fire.
Crackle! Crackle! Crackle!
But it did not burn up!

Moses went closer.
God spoke to him,

"Take off your shoes, Moses!
You are on holy ground."
Moses obeyed.

Then God said, "I am the God of
Abraham and Isaac and Jacob.
I have heard my people in Egypt
cry over and over for help.
Go, Moses, bring my people
out of Egypt."

"Who me?" said Moses.
"Yes, you," answered God.
"But what will I do there?"
said Moses.
"Tell Pharaoh to let my people go,"
God answered.
"Who me?" Moses said again.

"Yes, you," God answered again.

"But Pharaoh won't listen to me," said Moses. "Who can I say sent me?"

"Tell Pharaoh I AM sent you," answered God.

"Who me?" Moses said yet another time.

"Yes, you," God answered yet another time.

"But I can't speak well," said Moses.

"I will help you," said God.

"Your brother Aaron can speak for you."

"But—," said Moses.

"Go to Egypt, Moses!" God shouted.

Moses obeyed. He finally said yes

to God.

And together they did things

that have never been forgotten.

(Exodus 2: 11—Exodus 4: 17)

Hard-hearted Pharaoh

Moses did as God told him.

He and his brother, Aaron, went

to see Pharaoh.

Moses said to Pharaoh, "God says,

'Let my people go.'"

Hardhearted Pharaoh laughed.

"Ha! Ha! Ha!"

He folded his arms.

He stamped his foot.

He shouted, "I do not know your God.

So I will not obey him.

I will not let the Hebrew slaves go!"

"See the power of God," Moses said.

Aaron threw down Moses' staff.

It became a snake.

"Ha! Ha! Ha! My magicians can

do the same thing," said Pharaoh.

And they did.

But Moses' snake ate up

the other snakes.

Hardhearted Pharaoh saw

God's power.

But still he would not obey.

The next day Pharaoh went
to the river.
Moses and Aaron went there, too.
Moses said to Pharaoh, "God says,
'Let my people go.' "

Hardhearted Pharaoh laughed again.
"Ha! Ha! Ha!"
He folded his arms.
He stamped his foot. He shouted,
"I do not know your God.
So I will not obey him.
I will not let the Hebrew slaves go."

Moses told Aaron to raise
Moses' staff.

The river turned to blood.

The water in Pharaoh's house turned
to blood.

The water in every cup turned
to blood.

"Phew-wee!" said the Egyptians.

"There is no water to drink!"

Seven days went by.

Moses and Aaron went back
to Pharaoh.

"God says, 'Let my people go,' "
said Moses.

Hardhearted Pharaoh laughed.

"Ha! Ha! Ha!"

He folded his arms.

He stamped his foot.

He shouted, "I do not know your God.

So I will not obey him.

I will not let the Hebrew slaves go!"

Moses told Aaron to hold the staff
over the water.

Croak! Croak! Croak!

Frogs jumped out of the water.

Frogs filled the land.

Croak! Croak! Croak!

There were frogs in the gardens.

There were frogs in the houses.

There were frogs in the kitchens.

There were frogs in the beds.

Hardhearted Pharaoh saw
God's power.
But still he would not obey.
Next God sent mosquitoes.

ZZZZZZZZZZzzzzzzzzzzzzzzZZZZZZZZZZ

They bit the Egyptians on their arms.
They bit the Egyptians on their legs.
They bit the Egyptians on their
feet and hands.

ZZZZZZZZZZzzzzzzzzzzzzzzZZZZZZZZZZ

Every house was filled with
mosquitoes.
Next God sent flies, flies, and more
flies . . .

Five more times hardhearted Pharaoh
saw God's power.

God sent sickness to the animals.

God made the Egyptians break out
in sores.

God sent hail and grasshoppers.
God kept the sun from shining
for three days.
But still hardhearted Pharaoh
would not obey.

Finally God said to Moses,
"Tell the Hebrews to put the blood
of lambs on their doors.
Tonight the first son of every
Egyptian will die.
Be ready to leave quickly."

That night death came
to the Egyptians.

But death did not come
to the Hebrews.
"Remember this night forever and
ever," Moses said.
Finally hardhearted Pharaoh
believed in God's power.
Finally he obeyed.
Finally he let God's people go.

(Exodus 5—13)

Look what you've done now, Moses

The Hebrew people were happy
to leave Egypt.
The Egyptians were happy
to see them leave.
"Take whatever you wish,"
said the Egyptians.
"But go . . . go and never come back."

God led the people by day
with a cloud.
God led the people by night
with a column of fire.
God led the people to the Red Sea.
They set up camp.

But, back in Egypt,

Pharaoh changed his mind.

"We have no more slaves," he said.

"Who will do our work?

Who will build our cities?"

Pharaoh's heart grew hard again.

He folded his arms.

He stamped his foot.

"I do not know the God of Moses.

So I will not obey him.

I will not let the Hebrew slaves go."

Pharaoh called his army.

"We will ride after those slaves!"

So Pharaoh's army rode to the Red

Sea.

When the Hebrew people saw the
army, they were afraid.
"Look what you've done now, Moses!"
they said. "We are going to die.
We should have stayed in Egypt."

Moses answered,
"Do not worry. God will help us.
He always has. And he always will."
And God did.

God told Moses to raise his staff
over the sea.
Moses obeyed.
The waters divided in the middle.

Each side rolled back.

A path lay across the Red Sea!

"See the power of the Lord!"

Moses cried.

The Hebrew slaves ran into the sea.

Waters rose on their right.

Waters rose on their left.

Swisssssh! Swisssssh! Swisssssh!

Men and women,

boys and girls,

walked across the Red Sea.

Pharaoh's army followed.

But Moses raised his staff.

The waters on their right fell down.

The waters on their left fell down.

The water fell on top of them.

Shooooooosssssshhhh!

The army drowned.

The Hebrew slaves were free!

God's cloud led the Hebrews

into the desert.

For three days the Hebrews could not
find water.

They became very angry.

"Look what you've done now, Moses!
We have no water. We will die.
We should have stayed in Egypt!"

Moses answered,
"Do not worry. God will help us.
He always has. And he always will."
And God did.
He showed Moses where there was
plenty of water.

Then God's cloud led the Hebrews
further into the desert.
When there was no food,
the people became very angry.
"Look what you've done now, Moses!
We have no food. We will die.
We should have stayed in Egypt!"
Moses answered,
"Do not worry. God will help us.
He always has. And he always will."
And God did.
Every morning God sent bread from
heaven. It was called manna.
The Hebrews were never hungry.

"God loves us," they said.

"He always has. And he always will."

(Exodus 13: 17—Exodus 14: 31)

Around and around in circles

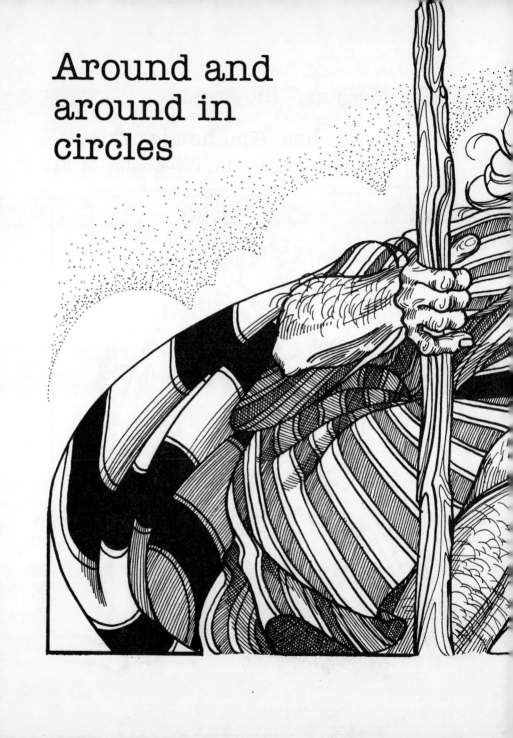

God's cloud led the Hebrews to

Mount Sinai.

Moses left them and went

up, up, up on the mountain top.

There God gave his laws to Moses.

YOU SHALL HAVE
NO OTHER GODS
BEFORE ME
YOU SHALL NOT
MAKE AN IDOL.

These were God's first two laws.

Moses stayed on the mountain

to hear God's many, many other laws.

Days went by.

The Hebrew people said,

"Maybe Moses is dead.

Let's make a golden cow.

It will be our god."

The Hebrews began to dance.

The Hebrews began to sing.

The Hebrews bowed down to the cow.

It was their idol.

God saw what the people were doing.

He said to Moses,

"Your people have done

a very bad thing.

They have made an idol.

I will kill them."

Moses asked God to forgive

his people.

"Remember Abraham and Isaac and

Jacob," Moses said.

"Please forgive their children."

And God did.

Then Moses went down the mountain.

He pulled down the golden cow.

"Those who are for the Lord,

come stand beside me," Moses said.

"Those who are for the golden cow, stay beside it."
Those who stood by the cow were killed right away.

Then Moses took the people away from Mount Sinai.
Soon they forgot how good God had been to them.
They said, "Look what you've done now, Moses!
We do not like manna.
We want meat to eat."

God heard them. He was angry.
But Moses asked God to forgive
them again. And God did.
He sent birds for them to eat.

At last, the Hebrews were
near Canaan,
the land promised to Abraham.
So Moses sent 12 men to look
at the land.
"Oh, oh," they cried when they
returned.
"The men who live in Canaan are big.
They are very, very big, indeed,"

the men said. "We will be killed
if we try to take the land."

But Joshua and Caleb were not afraid.

"God is on our side," they said.

"He will help us. He always has.

And he always will."

But the Hebrew people said,

"Look what you've done now, Moses.

We have no where to live.

We should go back to Egypt."

God heard the Hebrews. He was angry.

"Will these people ever believe in me?"

he asked. "I have helped them.

Still they do not believe in me.

Now I will kill them.

Then I will raise up a new nation."

Moses asked God to forgive

the Hebrews again.

But God was still very angry.

"I will keep the promise I made to
Abraham and Isaac and Jacob.
But *these* people will not see Canaan.
They will die here in the desert.
Only their children will go
into the promised land.
Joshua and Caleb will go, too,
because they believed."

So for 40 years the Hebrews
went around and around in circles.
They went this way and that way.
They went that way and this way.
But they never saw the promised land.

Before Moses died,

God allowed him to see Canaan.

Moses stood on the top of Mount Nebo.

He looked to the north and the south.

He looked to the east and the west.

"This is the land I promised to Abraham

and Isaac and Jacob," God said.

"I will give it to your children

and your children's children

from this time on."

(Exodus 15—Exodus 20;
Exodus 32—Exodus 33; Deuteronomy 34)